Grow It Yourself!

Grow Your Own Sandwich

John Malam

www.raintreepublishers.co.uk
Visit our website to find out
more information about
Raintree books.

To order:
☎ Phone 0845 6044371
🖹 Fax +44 (0) 1865 312263
🖳 Email myorders@raintreepublishers.co.uk

Customers from outside the UK please telephone +44 1865 312262

Raintree is an imprint of Capstone Global Library Limited,
a company incorporated in England and Wales having its
registered office at 7 Pilgrim Street, London, EC4V 6LB
– Registered company number: 6695582

Text © Capstone Global Library Limited 2012
First published in hardback in 2012
The moral rights of the proprietor have been asserted.

Edited by Daniel Nunn, Rebecca Rissman, and Sian Smith
Designed by Philippa Jenkins
Picture research by Mica Brancic
Production by Victoria Fitzgerald
Originated by Capstone Global Library Ltd
Printed and bound in China by Leo Paper Products Ltd

ISBN 978 1 406 22478 8
15 14 13 12 11
10 9 8 7 6 5 4 3 2 1

British Library Cataloguing in Publication Data
Malam, John, 1957-
Grow your own sandwich. -- (Grow it yourself!)
1. Salad vegetables--Juvenile literature. 2. Sandwiches--
Juvenile literature. 3. Gardening--Juvenile literature.
I. Title II. Series
635-dc22

Acknowledgements
The author and publisher are grateful to the following for
permission to reproduce copyright material: Alamy pp. 10 (©
FotoCraft), 12 (© David Pearson), 18, 19 (© 22DigiTal), 21
(© John Swithinbank); © Capstone Global Library Ltd pp. 13,
14, 15, 23 (Philippa Jenkins); © Capstone Publishers pp. 27,
28, 29 (Karon Dubke); Getty Images pp. 11 (Cultura/Nick
Daly), 20 (GAP Photos/Victoria Firmston), 22 (The Agency
Collection/PhotoConcepts); Shutterstock pp. 4 (© Grublee), 5
(© mocagrande), 6 (© SK Bakker), 7 (© Ruslan Semichev), 8
(© Palis Michalis), 9 (© Helen Shorey), 16 (© Dewitt), 17 (©
LianeM), 24 (© Mageon), 25 (© Samokhin), 26 (© Kzenon).

Background cover photograph of red tomatoes reproduced
with permission of Shutterstock (© Olegusk). Foreground cover
photograph reproduced with permission of © Capstone Global
Library Ltd (Philippa Jenkins).

Every effort has been made to contact copyright holders
of material reproduced in this book. Any omissions will
be rectified in subsequent printings if notice is given to the
publisher.

To find out about the author, visit his website:
www.johnmalam.co.uk

Disclaimer
All the Internet addresses (URLs) given in this book were valid
at the time of going to press. However, due to the dynamic
nature of the Internet, some addresses may have changed, or
sites may have changed or ceased to exist since publication.
While the author and Publishers regret any inconvenience this
may cause readers, no responsibility for any such changes can
be accepted by either the author or the Publishers.

Some words are shown in bold, **like this**. You can
find out what they mean by looking in the glossary.

Contents

Safety note:
It is important to always wash your hands carefully after handling tomato plants. Ask an adult to help you with the activities in this book.

What is a tomato?

A tomato is the **fruit** of the tomato plant. In the summer, tomato plants make lots of tasty tomatoes. They are good to eat, and can be used in many different ways.

A tomato can be as big as your hand!

Most tomatoes turn red when they are ready to pick.

Tomato plants are easy to grow. A few weeks after the tomato **seeds** have been **sown**, the plants make flowers. After a few days, baby tomatoes appear. When they are **ripe**, they are ready to pick.

Shapes, sizes, and seeds

There are many types of tomato. Some are as small as cherries, and some are as big as oranges. They can be round, oval, or flattened.

Tomato skins can be smooth, bumpy, or striped.

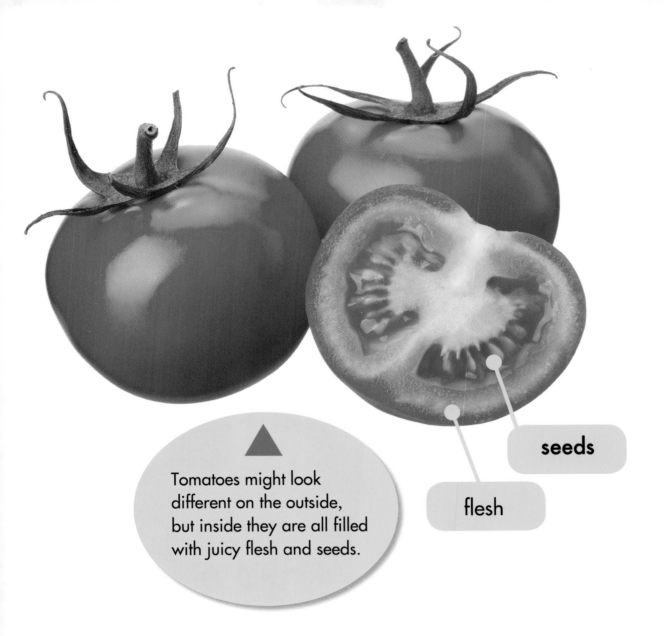

seeds

flesh

Tomatoes might look different on the outside, but inside they are all filled with juicy flesh and seeds.

There are red, purple, yellow, and orange tomatoes. Each type has a name, such as Gardener's Delight, Red Cherry, or Mr Stripey.

Tall and short plants

Tomato plants can be tall or short. Tall plants grow to more than 2 metres high. They have one main **stem** and need a cane to lean against for support. They are known as **cordon tomatoes**.

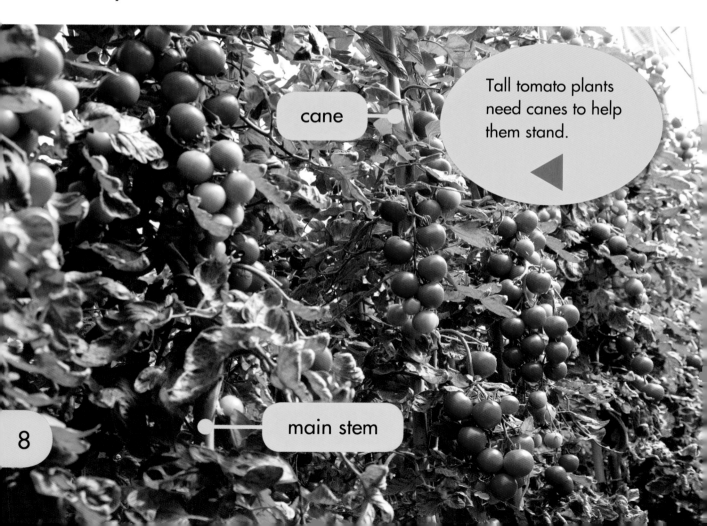

cane

Tall tomato plants need canes to help them stand.

main stem

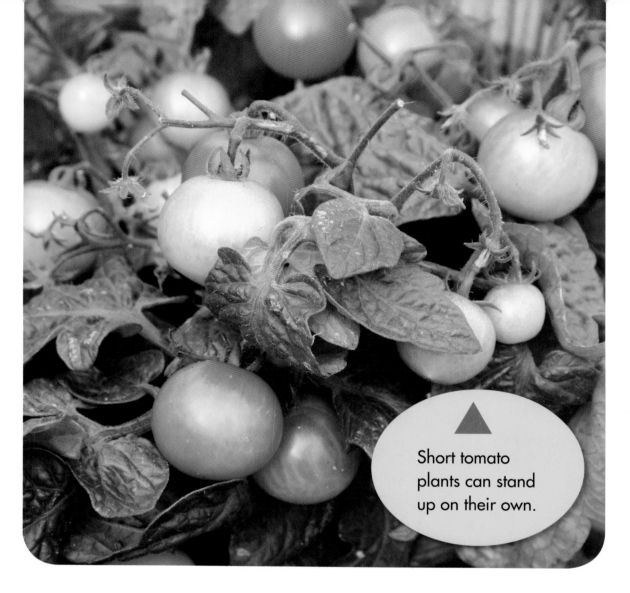

Short tomato plants can stand up on their own.

Short tomato plants are less than 1 metre high. They have lots of stems, and are known as **bush tomatoes**. Dwarf tomato plants are shorter still. They are only about 20 centimetres high.

Where to grow

Tomato plants grow in many different places. Some like to be outside in gardens, vegetable beds, plant pots, or hanging baskets. They like a sunny spot, sheltered from the wind.

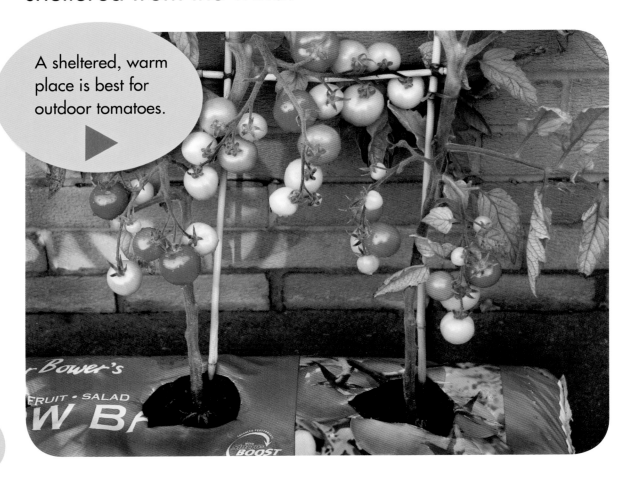

A sheltered, warm place is best for outdoor tomatoes. ▶

Tomatoes grow very well inside a polytunnel, where it is warm.

Some tomato plants prefer to be kept very warm, so they are grown inside **greenhouses** or **polytunnels**. These buildings stay warm all day long, and even through the night.

Get ready to grow!

Garden centres have everything you need for growing tomato plants. Some shops and supermarkets also sell the same equipment.

To grow your own tomato plants, you will need a packet of tomato **seeds**. Choose an upright **cordon** type, such as Gardener's Delight.

These are just some of the varieties of tomato you can choose from.

watering rose

You will also need: seed **compost**, a seed tray, small plant pots (about 8 centimetres wide), large plant pots (about 25 centimetres wide) or a **growing bag**, labels, garden **twine**, bamboo canes (about 1½ metres high), a watering can with a **watering rose**, and liquid tomato feed.

Sowing the seeds

1. In February or March, fill the **seed** tray with seed **compost**.
2. Lay out the tomato seeds on top of the compost, putting one seed in each cell.
3. Gently push each seed down into the compost, about 1½ centimetres deep.

plant label

4. Sprinkle a little more compost over the tray to cover the seeds.

5. Add a label with the name of the tomatoes and the date you **sowed** them.

6. Water the tray, then leave it in a warm place indoors. Don't let it dry out!

Potting on

After about ten days, tiny shoots will appear. When the **seedlings** are about 5 centimetres tall, they are ready to "pot on" into the small pots.

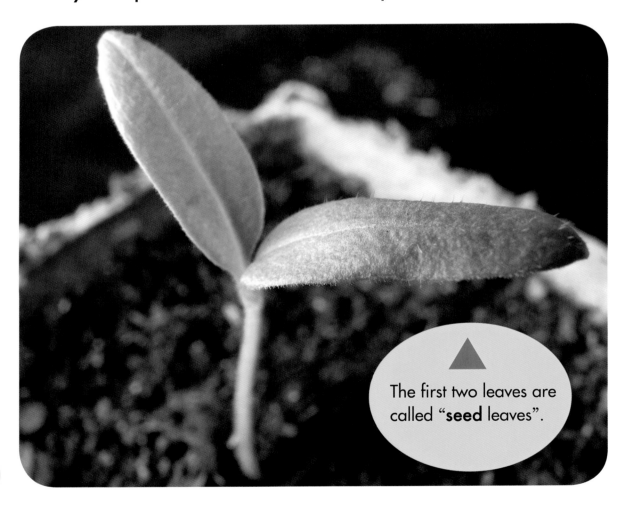

The first two leaves are called "**seed** leaves".

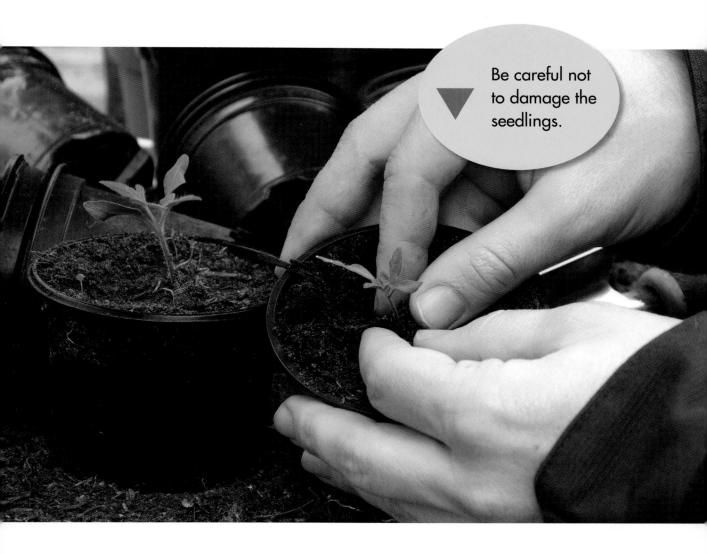

Be careful not to damage the seedlings.

Fill the pots with **compost** and make deep holes in the centres. Put one seedling into each pot. Press the compost down around the seedlings. Keep the compost moist, but not too wet.

Planting out

The **seedlings** will grow into small tomato plants. When they are about 20 centimetres high, they will be ready to **plant out** into their final growing places.

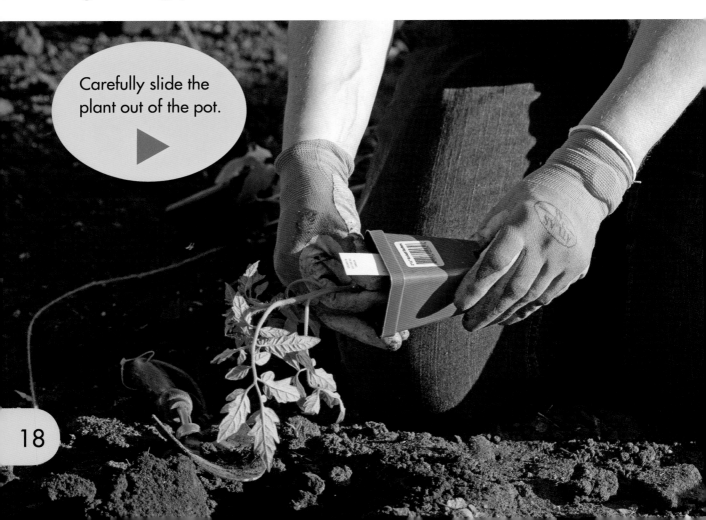

Carefully slide the plant out of the pot.

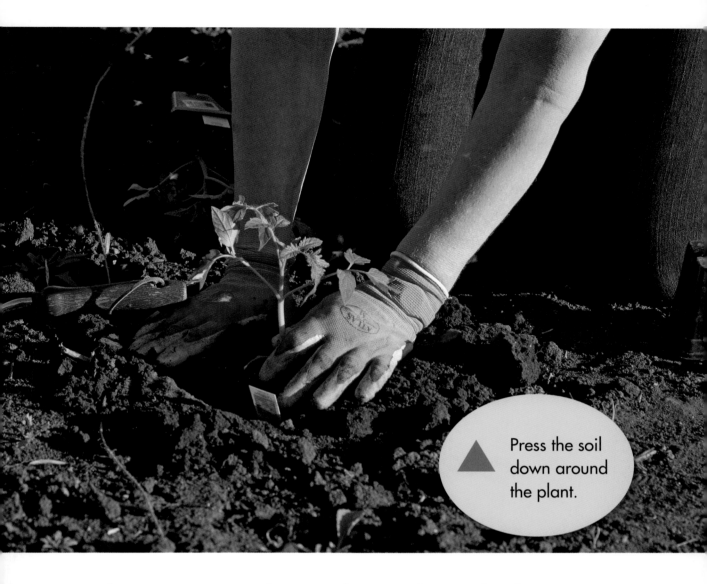

Press the soil down around the plant.

Turn the pots on to their sides and tap the bottoms. The plants and the **compost** should slide out. Put the plants into holes in the ground, or into large pots filled with compost, or **growing bags**.

Caring for your plants

The plants will grow quickly. To stop them falling over, put a 1½ metre bamboo cane next to each one. Tie the **stems** to the canes with garden **twine**.

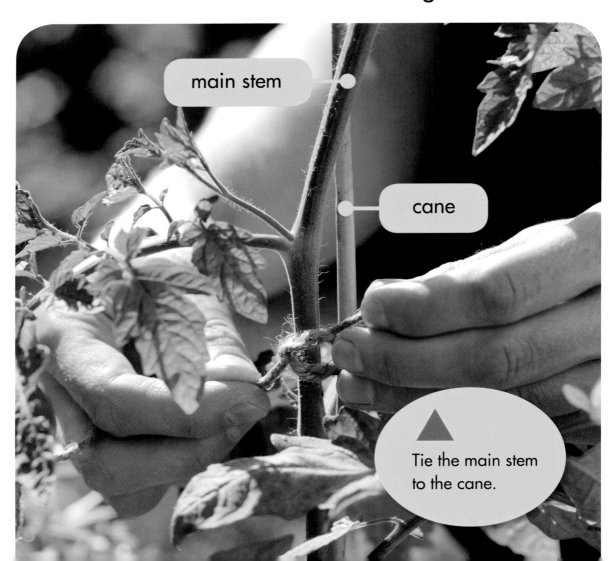

main stem

cane

Tie the main stem to the cane.

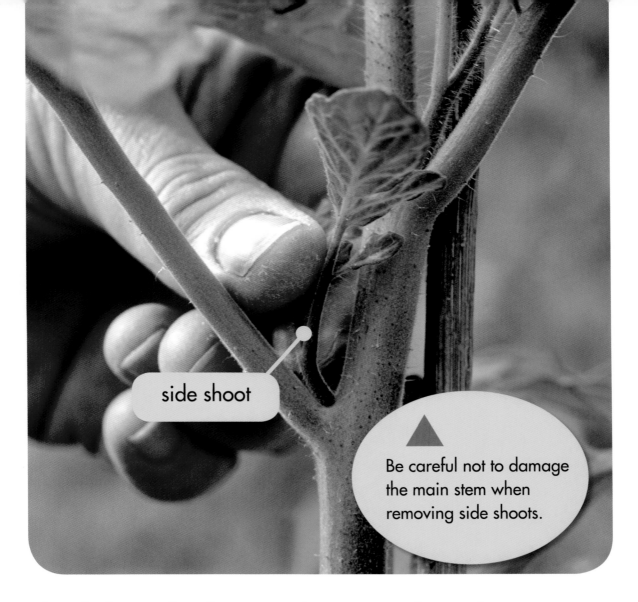

side shoot

Be careful not to damage the main stem when removing side shoots.

Check for **side shoots**. They grow from the main stem, close to where a leaf joins it. Side shoots take energy away from the plant. Pinch out or snap off the side shoots.

Watering and feeding

Keep the plants well watered. Plants in the ground need watering too, especially if it hasn't rained for a few days.

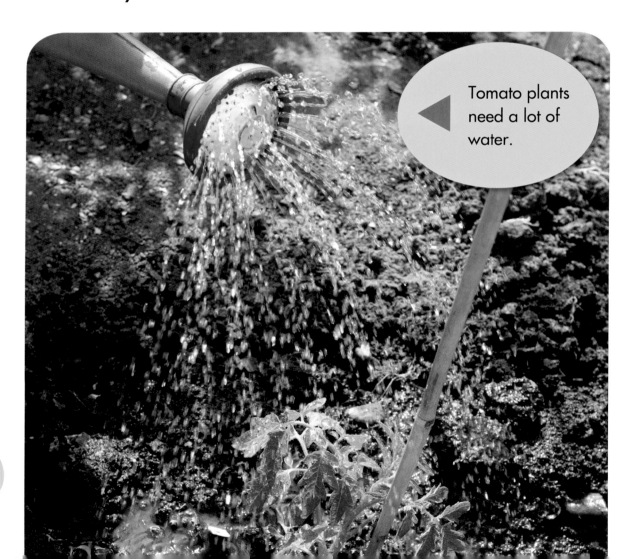

Tomato plants need a lot of water.

Instructions on the liquid feed will tell you how much to use.

Tomato plants are hungry. Once a week, give them a feed. Mix a liquid tomato feed into their water. It contains all the **nutrients** they need.

From flower to fruit

In June, yellow flowers appear. The flowers make yellow **pollen**. The wind moves the pollen from flower to flower, and when this happens the tomatoes start to grow.

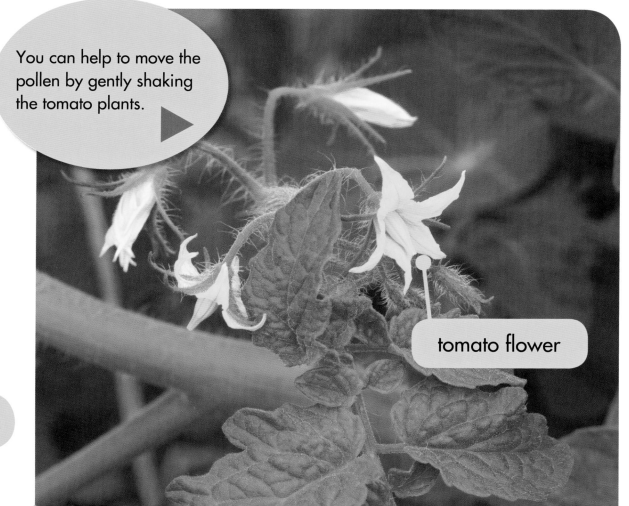

You can help to move the pollen by gently shaking the tomato plants. ▶

tomato flower

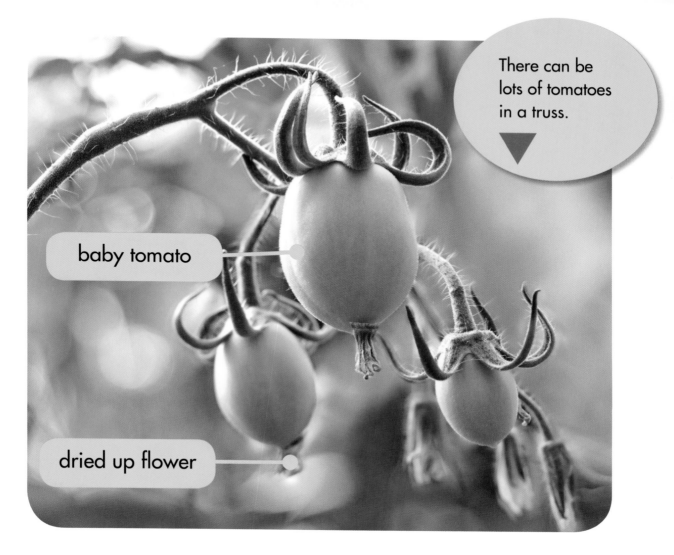

There can be lots of tomatoes in a truss.

baby tomato

dried up flower

The flowers last a few days, then tiny green "beads" start to grow. These are baby tomatoes. They swell quickly until they have grown into full-sized tomatoes. A bunch of tomatoes is called a **truss**.

Tasty tomatoes!

Ripe tomatoes are red, purple, yellow, or orange. To pick them, hold them gently and snap them off the **truss**. Have a sniff – they will smell fresh. Have a taste – they will be sweet and juicy.

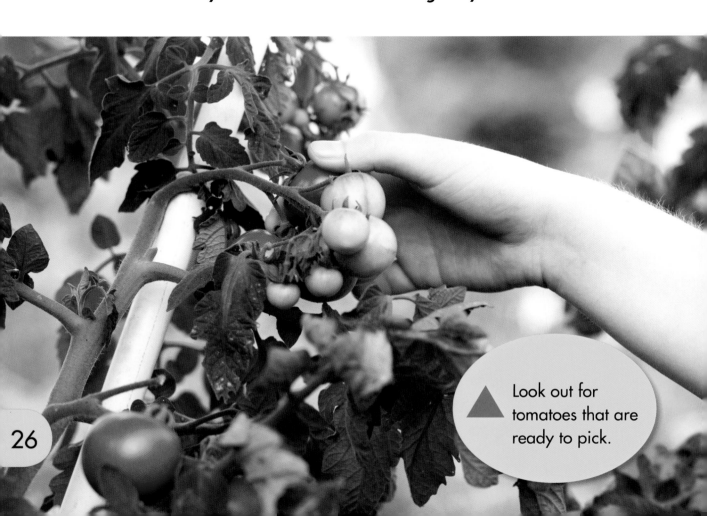

Look out for tomatoes that are ready to pick.

26

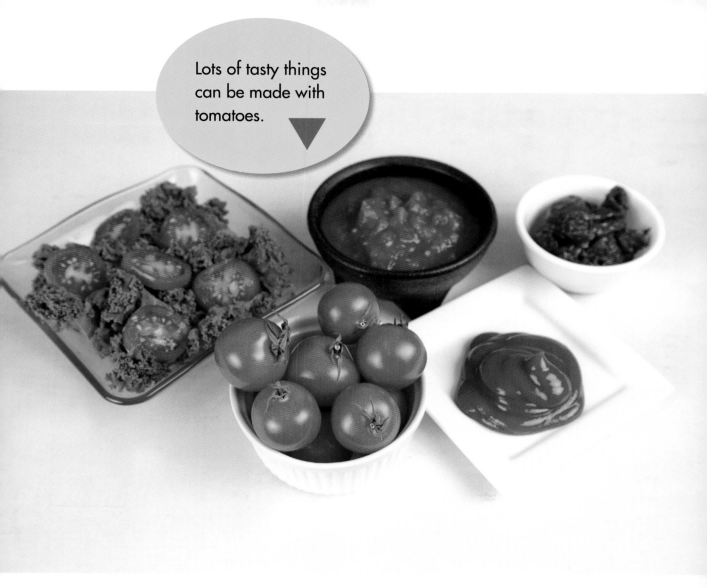

Lots of tasty things can be made with tomatoes.

Tomatoes are good for you. They can be eaten **raw** in salads and sandwiches. They can be made into sauces and soups, pickles and chutneys. They can be roasted, grilled, baked, fried, and dried.

Make a cheese and tomato sandwich

You will need: 2 or 3 **ripe** tomatoes, cheese, 2 pieces of sliced bread, margarine, and lettuce.

1. Cut the tomatoes and the cheese into thin slices.
2. Spread margarine onto two pieces of bread.
3. Put the cheese slices onto the bread.
4. Put the tomato slices on top of the cheese.

5. Add lettuce to the sandwich if you wish.
6. Put one slice of bread on top of the other.
7. Cut your sandwich in half or leave it whole. Eat and enjoy!

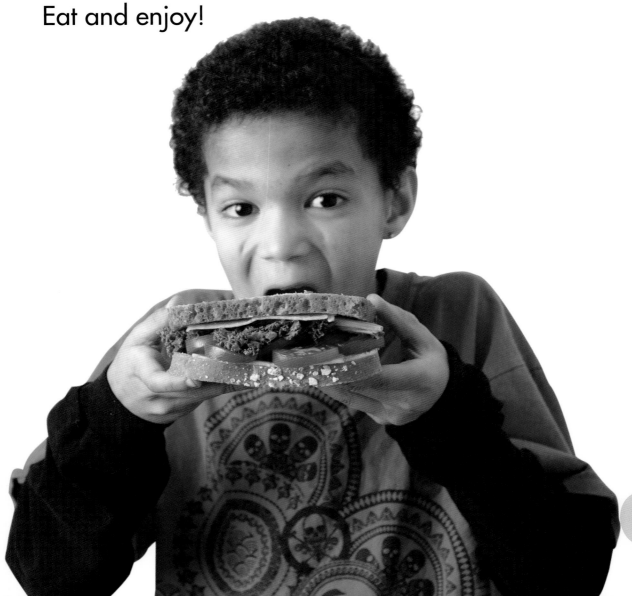

Glossary

bush tomato short tomato plant with several bushy stems

compost loose, earthy material used for growing seeds and plants

cordon tomato tall tomato plant with one main stem

fruit the part of a plant which can often be eaten as food. Fruit contains seeds.

greenhouse a building with glass sides and a glass roof

growing bag a special bag filled with compost

nutrients substances that help to keep plants healthy

plant out when a plant is planted into its final growing place

pollen tiny powdery grains made by flowers

polytunnel a building with metal hoops covered in a sheet of thick polythene

raw food that has not been cooked

ripe fully grown and ready to pick or eat

seed the part of a plant that grows into a new plant

seedling a baby plant

side shoots shoots that grow from the side of a plant's main stem

sow to plant a seed

sown to have planted a seed

stem the main branch or trunk of a plant

truss a bunch of tomatoes growing on a tomato plant

twine a type of string used in gardens

watering rose a sprinkler on the end of a watering can

Find out more

Books to read

Grow It, Eat It, D. K. Publishing (Dorling Kindersley, 2008)

Ready, Steady, Grow!, Royal Horticultural Society (Dorling Kindersley, 2010)

Tomatoes (Grow Your Own), Helen Lanz (Franklin Watts, 2010)

Websites

www.gardenersworld.com/how-to/projects/tomatoes-seeds-grow/

This website shows you a different way to grow tomatoes from seed and includes a helpful video to watch.

www.kiddiegardens.com

This site will give you lots of ideas on how to grow plants that you can use to make things.

www.thekidsgarden.co.uk

Discover more gardening ideas and activities on this website.

Index

Newport Community Learning & Libraries
Cymuned ddysgu a Llyfrgelloedd Casnewydd

THIS ITEM SHOULD BE RETURNED OR
RENEWED BY THE LAST DATE
STAMPED BELOW

Newport
CITY COUNCIL
CYNGOR DINAS
Casnewydd

J

To renew telephone 656656 or 656657 (minicom)
or www.newport.gov.uk/libraries